Devotionals for families with young children
by William L. Coleman

Counting Stars, meditations on God's creation.

My Magnificent Machine, devotionals centered around the marvels of the human body.

Listen to the Animals, lessons from the animal world.

On Your Mark, challenges from the lives of well-known athletes.

✓*The Good Night Book*, bedtime inspirationals (especially for those who may be afraid of the dark).

✓The Sleep Tight Book
✓Today I feEl like a Warm fuzzy
✓TodayI feel loved

The Good Night Book

William L. Coleman

Bethany Fellowship INC.
MINNEAPOLIS, MINNESOTA 55438

Biographical Sketch

WILLIAM L. COLEMAN is a graduate of the Washington Bible College in Washington, D.C., and Grace Theological Seminary in Winona Lake, Indiana.

He has pastored three churches: a Baptist church in Michigan, a Mennonite church in Kansas, and an Evangelical Free Church in Aurora, Nebraska. He is a Staley Foundation lecturer.

The author of 75 magazine articles, his by-line has appeared in *Christianity Today, Eternity, Good News Broadcaster, Campus Life, Moody Monthly, Evangelical Beacon,* and *The Christian Reader.*

This is his fifth children's book.

Copyright © 1979
William L. Coleman

Published by Bethany Fellowship, Inc.
6820 Auto Club Road, Minneapolis, Minnesota 55438

Printed in the United States of America

Library of Congress Cataloging in Publication Data

Coleman, William L.
    The good night book.

    SUMMARY: Brief passages reveal the handiwork of God occurring at night, both in nature and in our homes. Biblical quotations follow each passage.
    1. Children—prayer-books and devotions—English.
[1. Prayer books and devotions]   I.   Title.
BV4870.C632   242'.62   79-20002
ISBN 0-87123-187-5

Dedicated to

Michael and John Coleman

Contents

Nights
Are Great!

Nights are packed full
of feelings, sounds, adventures
and even beautiful colors.
This book will tell you
just a few of the interesting
things which go on.

Night can be our friend.
We should get to know it better.
While we are at it,
we can learn about our God
who rules over the night.

William L. Coleman
Aurora, Nebraska

Going to Sleep

What is it like to go to sleep?
Do you go to sleep quickly?
Does your body slow down
A little at a time?

For most of us sleep comes slowly.
While we are lying down,
Our muscles start to relax.
Our arms and legs stop moving around.

Soon our mind slows down.
We won't be able to think as well.
Our eyelids will seem heavy
And our eyes will keep closing.

You may not know it,
But your heart will beat slower, too.
You are almost asleep now.

A warm cover will be a good idea.
Your body temperature will get lower.
Without a cover you will probably get chilly.
Breathe deeply, now.
Good night.

"He giveth his beloved sleep"
(Ps. 127:2, KJV).

Falling Stars

On some nights you can see fire
Falling from the sky.
We usually call this falling stars.
They aren't really stars but meteors.

Meteors are made of stone or iron.
They break loose from bigger pieces in the sky.

Every night thousands of meteors break off.
Many start heading for earth.
Before they get here
They catch fire and burn up.

A few meteors hit the earth
But not many.
Because they burn up in the sky
We are safe and can sleep quietly.

They are fun to watch.
A large shower of them
Come down in November.
Some museums have meteors to see.

The skies are busy
Showing the creation of God.

"The heavens are telling the glory of God; they are a marvelous display of his craftsmanship" (Ps. 19:1, TLB).

The Wet Grass

While you are sleeping tonight
Nature will be hard at work.

When you get up tomorrow
The grass will probably be wet,
And yet it may not have rained.

The wet on the grass is called dew.
During the night the grass becomes cool.
When air touches the grass
Little pieces of water form.

If the night is too cold,
The water will freeze on the grass.
This is called frost.

In the desert there isn't much rain.
The dew at night is a big help.
By supplying water, the grass and plants
Are kept alive.

While you are sleeping tonight,
Nature will be hard at work.

Job thanked God for the dew.

**"For everything I did prospered;
the dew lay all night upon my fields
and watered them"** (Job 29:19, TLB).

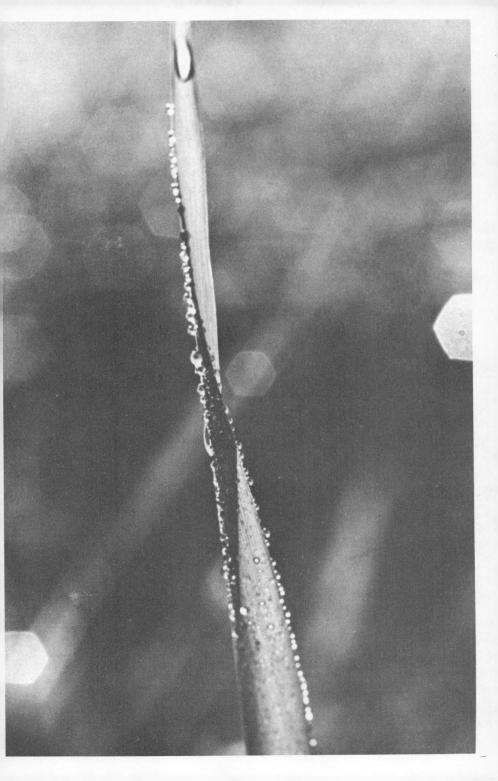

The Birds Go to Bed

The birds are doing the same thing
You are right now.

They are getting ready for bed.
Some look for a nest, others eat.

A few are arguing over where to sleep.

Many birds like to sing.
Sparrows sing for 15 minutes before bed.
After it is dark the robin keeps on singing.
Sometimes its song takes an hour.

The swallows want more food.
They pick a few more insects.

It is quiet now.
The birds have gone to bed.

"Then my nights are filled with joyous songs" (Ps. 77:6, TLB).

The Sun Is Waiting

When you wake up tomorrow
The sun will be coming up in the east.

Even if it is raining or foggy
And the skies are dark,
The sun will still be there
Whether you can see it or not.

We say the sun "comes up,"
But it doesn't really.
It just looks that way.

The earth goes around the sun,
The sun doesn't go around the earth.
It just looks that way.

The sun is really much bigger
Than the earth.
The earth would fit inside the sun
One million times.

The earth is spinning around
Like a top.
The sun is spinning also.

When you wake up tomorrow morning
The sun will be waiting for you,
Even if you don't see it.

**"Day and night alike belong to you;
you made the starlight and the sun"**
(Ps. 74:16, TLB).

Is the Moon Out?

Many nights when we are sleeping,
The moon shines outside our window.

It looks like the moon is close to us.
The truth is, it is almost 250,000 miles away.

The moon has a beautiful yellow-orange color.
We wouldn't be able to see it,
But the sun shines its light like a flashlight.
This light shines on the moon
And lets us see it.

In 1969 the first man
Walked on the moon.

There is no other life there—
No people, no animals, no plants, no bugs.

Some nights we can't see the moon,
But it is out there.
The moon keeps moving around the world.

While you sleep tonight,
The moon will keep moving around.

"The moon and stars to rule by night: for his mercy endureth forever"
(Ps. 136:9, KJV).

How Many Stars?

If the night sky were as clear
As it could be,
We could count 2,000 stars.
But we can't see most of them.

Scientists tell us there are more stars
Than all the grains of sand
On all the beaches
In all the world.

The earth lives in a group of stars.
They are called the Milky Way.

The sun is a star,
But we see it in the daytime.

On some nights the stars look close,
But don't plan on taking a trip to one.
The nearest star is millions of miles away.

God is so great
He knows every star by name.
He also knows you.

"He counts the stars and calls them all by name" (Ps. 147:4, TLB).

A Night Flower

While you are sleeping tonight,
The yellow evening primrose will wake up.

During the night this pretty plant
Wiggles its petals open.

The moths and night flies
Will see it in the darkness.
They find the primroses
By the country road
And use them for food.

If you listened carefully,
You could hear little popping noises
As they open.

When you wake up tomorrow,
They will be closed again.

"He sends the night and darkness, when all the forest folk come out"
(Ps. 104:20, TLB).

When Does God Sleep?

Everyone we know needs sleep.
Many need six or eight hours.
Most children get around ten hours.

But when does God sleep?
Does He have a bed?
Or does He sleep on a cloud?

Does God take a nap?
Does He go to sleep in a big chair
Like Mom and Dad sometimes do?

God is so strong
He doesn't need any of these.
God never has to go to sleep.

While you are sleeping tonight,
God will stay awake,
And He will watch you
With His love.

"He is always watching, never sleeping" (Ps. 121:4, TLB).

Holding
Each Other

Have you seen pictures of monkeys
With their arms wrapped around each other?
Have you seen baby chicks resting
Under their mother's wings?

Animals like to touch and hold each other.
It is a warm and loving feeling.

You probably enjoy the same thing.
Can you remember sitting on someone's lap?
Do you like having someone read to you?
Have you ever gone to sleep
In someone's arms?

It feels so good because you know
Someone loves you.

Parents enjoy being held, too.
They feel loved when someone puts his arms
Around them and gives them a big hug.
They also like a kiss
That says, "I really like you."

Can you remember walking with a parent
And holding his hand
While you talked?
It made both of you feel better.

Before you go to sleep tonight
Give someone a gigantic hug.
Don't forget a kiss, too.
Both of you will feel loved.

"But even so, you love me! You are holding my right hand!" (Ps. 73:23, TLB).

Flying Lights

They fly around the yard every summer.
Some children catch them.
When put in bottles they make good lights.
They are called lightning bugs or fireflies.

During the day fireflies sleep.
At night they shake their wings loose
And fly.

They have small lamps next to their stomach.
Their light gets brighter
When they breathe in.

Their light helps them find each other.

If a firefly gets into trouble,
It breathes hard
And the lamp becomes extra bright.

Like the firefly we have a light.
The Bible works like a flashlight.
It shows us how to stay out of trouble.

"For even darkness cannot hide from God" (Ps. 139:12, TLB).

No More Nights

It happens every day—
Daylight comes and goes,
And then it gets dark.
Night always follows day.

Can you imagine a day
When night did not come?
It stayed light all night long.

Then, the next day would come,
But it stayed, too.
Suppose we did not need night anymore?

The Bible tells us a time will come
When there will be no more night.
We will live with God,
And there will be no darkness.

I wonder what that will be like.
There probably won't be any more sleep
Because we won't need it.

There will be no pain.
No crying. No tears.
No sorrow. No one will die.

Living with God and Jesus Christ
Will change our lives completely—
Both day and night.

"And there will be no night there—no
need for lamps or sun—for the Lord
God will be their light; and they shall
reign forever and ever" (Rev. 22:5, TLB).

Raccoons Enjoy the Night

A raccoon looks like a robber.
He has small black spots
Around his eyes.
It looks like a mask.

Nighttime doesn't slow the raccoon.
It can see well in the dark.
During the night they catch fish.
You can hear them splashing in the river.

Sometimes they visit campers.
Raccoons like to turn over garbage cans
And eat the food we did not finish.

Before morning they sneak away.
Tomorrow night they will be back.

"God made all sorts of wild animals and cattle and reptiles, and God was pleased with what he had done"
(Gen. 1:25, TLB).

Do You Dream?

Did you ever wake up and wish you hadn't?
You were having a terrific dream
And you wanted to roll over and finish it.

Maybe you were dreaming about a game
You were playing.
Or you had just received
A large dish of ice cream.

I can remember dreams that frightened me.
I would wake up scared
And not want to go back to sleep.

All of us have dreams.
We see pictures in our minds
And even think we are talking to someone.

Some dreams seem so real
We aren't sure if they really happened or not.

Dreams have never hurt anyone.
Most of the time we forget them.
Sometimes they are so interesting
We remember them for a long time.

Can you remember a dream you enjoyed?

Each morning the dreams all go away.
But someone never goes away.
God has watched you all night.
The minute you wake up He is by your side.

"Then I lay down and slept in peace and woke up safely, for the Lord was watching over me" (Ps. 3:5, TLB).

Do You Ever Get Scared?

Are you ever afraid
And you haven't told anyone
What scares you?

Most of us get that way sometimes.
We are afraid of a big dog
That lives down the street and barks at us.

Some of us are afraid of the big road
In front of our house.
There is reason to be afraid.
The cars and trucks can be dangerous.

I am afraid of real high places.
I don't like to look down
Because it makes my stomach feel funny.

Are you ever afraid of getting lost?
One of my children walked away
From a house we were visiting.
She got lost and couldn't find the house again.
We finally found her.

Sometimes are you afraid of the dark?
Do you ever hear noises and wonder
What they are?

It would be a help if you could tell someone
What frightens you.

Maybe you can talk to your parents,
A big brother, or a teacher.

Another person we can tell is Jesus Christ.
He wants to know what makes us happy
And what makes us afraid.
Jesus really cares what happens in your life.

"Let him have all your worries and cares, for he is always thinking about you and watching everything that concerns you" (1 Pet. 5:7, TLB).

The Dark Ocean

When the light is turned off,
Your room becomes very dark.

There may be some light
From another room or a night-light.
But mostly the room is dark.

There is one place where it is dark all the time.

The bottom of the ocean has no light.
It is seven miles to the deepest part.
It is always night there.

It is so dark the small fish
Have lights on their bodies.
They look like tiny flashlights.
Some fish are covered with lights
Like Christmas trees.

In a dark room, a dark forest,
Or a dark ocean
God can see us.

**"Your words are a flashlight to light
the path ahead of me, and keep me
from stumbling"** (Ps. 119:105, TLB).

What Did You Learn?

Life is so interesting.
The more we learn about our world
The more exciting life is.
What did you learn today?
Did you know there is a full-grown deer
Which only becomes one-foot high?

Did you know a camel can eat a thorny cactus
And chew it without hurting its mouth?

Did you know that in a land called Tibet
They use butter for money?

Did you know there are around
250 bones in your body?

Did you know that no one sounds
The same way you do?

Did you know your blood travels
Through your body
600 times every day?

Did you know Jesus Christ was alive
Long before the world was made?

Did you know Jesus will come back someday?
But we aren't sure when.

Did you know Jesus has made
A place for you in heaven?

There are so many things to learn.
Don't forget to learn about Jesus Christ, too.

"Learn of me" (Matt. 11:29, KJV).

Bedtime

Have you ever watched other children
At bedtime?

Some behave very nicely.
When their parents tell them to go to bed,
They put their things away and start going.

Other children do just the opposite.
They get out more toys,
Or they keep on watching television.
Once in a while a child will even hide.

Have you seen other children
Who have to be told over and over again?
They make it hard for their parents.
They are also learning bad habits.

God knows children need their parents.
They need clean clothes and good food.
Children also need to be told what to do
Until they are old enough to tell themselves.

Most children don't like to go to bed.
You go when you are told
Because your parents know what is best.

Thank God for parents.

**"Young man, obey your father and
your mother"** (Prov. 6:20, TLB).

Grasshopper Mouse

Most mice eat corn, wheat and seeds.
In someone's house
They could eat many foods,
Including fruit.

Tonight some mice are looking
For different food.
They are searching for grasshoppers.

The grasshopper mouse lives in the west.
They like the dry deserts.
Sometimes they like worms or insects.
Most of the time they chase grasshoppers.

This mouse has to be quiet.
That is why night is his best time.
They sneak up on a grasshopper
Like a soft-footed cat.

In one month a grasshopper mouse
Can give birth to four baby mice.

They are afraid of people,
So they don't bother children.

"And out of the ground the Lord God formed every beast of the field"
(Gen. 2:19, KJV).

Kangaroos at Night

If you lived in Australia
Far away from the cities,
You might hear a strange noise at night.
It could be the hopping kangaroos
Jumping across the open fields.

Kangaroos come out during the day,
But they enjoy the night better.
Usually they travel in groups.
There might be only a few,
Or there could be a hundred together.

A mother kangaroo has a pouch
Across her stomach.
It looks like a mother's purse.
A baby kangaroo lives here
Until it is two years old and quite large.

If a baby kangaroo goes away,
It could be in trouble.
Eagles try to pick them off the ground.
Big lizards try to get the smallest ones.

Usually it is the baby "roos"
Who disobey
Who get themselves hurt.
If they stay close to the pouch
Their mother can always protect them.

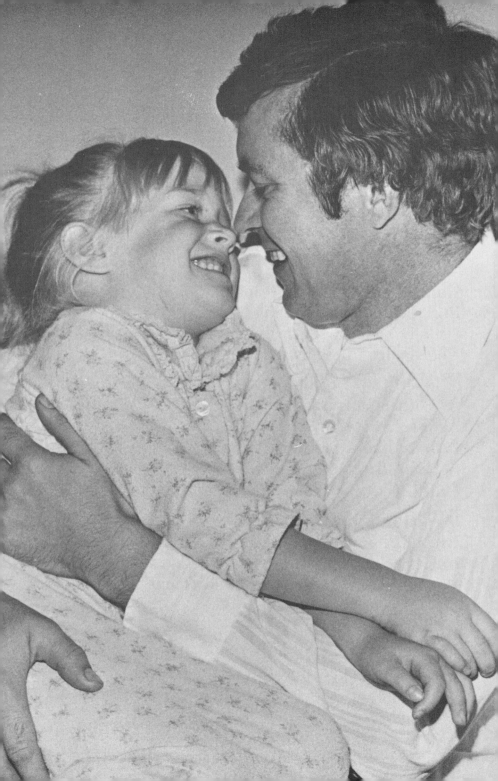

They are like children who do the same thing.
God told us to obey our parents.
He knew they could take the best care of you—
Both day and night.

"Children, obey your parents; this is the right thing to do because God has placed them in authority over you" (Eph. 6:1, TLB).

Snug As a Bug

When someone is sleeping quietly,
We often say
He is as snug as a bug in a rug.

But how snug is a bug?
Where do they sleep?
Do they lie flat?
Curl into a ball?
Or hang from a tree?

Some insects look for a dark, quiet place.
They land inside a flower
Which closes for the night.
You might find them inside
A pretty little poppy.

If you were a wasp, you would use your teeth.
They bite into a plant and lay across the stem.
A wasp's feet hang over and dangle loose.
They sleep in comfort all night.

Butterflies look for a place to hide.
Often they spend the night in thick grass
Or deep in the weeds.
In the morning butterflies and moths
Will fly out of the grass as you walk along.

Ants are different.
They not only sleep at night,
Often they take a nap in the afternoon.

If you watch carefully, you might see
An ant yawn and stretch just like a person.

Your bed is more comfortable
Than hanging from a tree.
Your pillow is softer
Than sleeping inside a flower.

God watches over your soft bed.
All night long He loves you.
Think about Him while you go to sleep.

"When I remember thee upon my bed, and meditate on thee in the night watches" (Ps. 63:6, KJV).

Flying Squirrels

After you go to sleep tonight
The flying squirrels will come out
And start searching for food.

Most of us have never seen a flying squirrel.
This is because they enjoy the forest
And the dark.
Around 11 o'clock on a warm night
They poke their heads out.
By 2 a.m. they are finished and go back home.

They use these three hours
To teach their young.
Each baby squirrel will have to learn
To hunt and stay away from danger.

A flying squirrel sails like a kite.
He stretches his arms and legs out.
There is extra skin between them
To catch the air.
He can sail 150 feet from one tree to the next.

If we could spend a night in the forest
With our parents
And we could see in the dark,
We might be amazed at what God has created.

Little animals and big ones.
Fast animals and slow ones,
That waddle when they walk.

But God's most amazing creation is people
Just like you.
You are really special to God.
He wanted someone
Exactly like you.

"O Lord, what a variety you have made! And in wisdom you have made them all! The earth is full of your riches" (Ps. 104:24, TLB).

The Police Stay Awake

We live in a small town.
Late at night almost everyone is in bed.

It is a quiet place to live.
There is almost no trouble at night.

But sometimes I wonder
What would happen
If there were a fire or someone became sick
In the middle of the night.

In our town there is a man
Who works all night at the sheriff's office.
If anything goes wrong we can just call him.
He is called a "Dispatcher."

The minute the Dispatcher gets a call
He calls the police, the fireman
Or the ambulance.
Any of them can be at our house
In a few minutes.

There is also a policeman who drives
Around our town all night.
If he sees anyone having trouble,
He is right there to help.

Our hospital is open all night.
Nurses are always taking care of patients.
It would take only five minutes to get there.
If we need a doctor, he can be there
Quickly, too.

Our firemen are fast.
If the Dispatcher calls them,
They can get to our house in a hurry.

It is good to know these people are awake
Or close by.
We sleep well knowing there are people
Who care.

God knew we would need policemen,
Doctors and firemen.
Tonight you can sleep better
Because they are around.

"The policeman is sent by God to help you" (Rom. 13:4, TLB).

The Howler Monkey

What do most children
Want to see at the zoo?
More than any place else
They stop in front of the monkey cages.

One interesting little animal
Is called the Howler Monkey.
He is named the Howler
Because this is what he does.
He howls in a loud and scary voice.

He only weighs a few pounds
But can make a noise to frighten
Almost anyone.

The Howler Monkey's yell sounds like
The roar of a lion,
And it can be heard a mile away.

If he thinks trouble is coming,
He merely starts to yell.
Most animals and people
Soon go the other way.

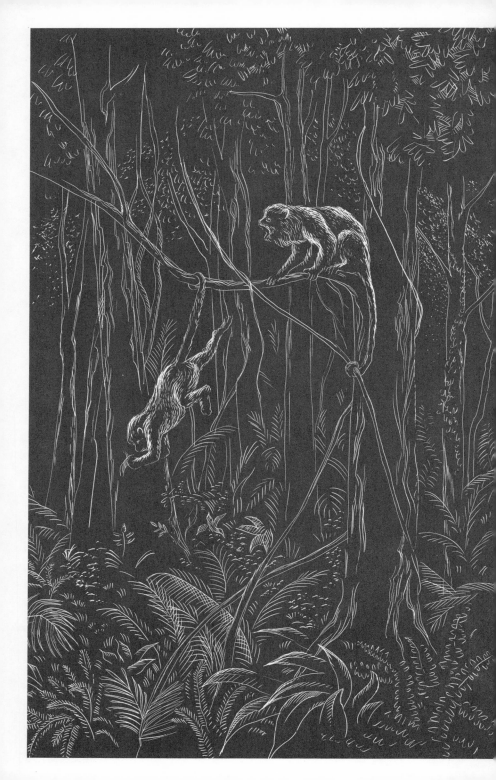

A Howler Monkey knows when to be noisy.
Does he also know when to be quiet?
When it's bedtime, does he calm down
And let the other monkeys go to sleep?

The Bible tells me there is a time
To make noise.
It also says there is a time to be quiet.
Bedtime is the time to whisper and then
Be quiet!! Good night!

"A time to be quiet; a time to speak up" (Eccles. 3:7, TLB).

Pick Out Your Covers

Are your covers ready for the night?
Why do you get covered up anyway?
If your house is warm,
Do you really need covers?

When you go to sleep tonight,
Something special will happen to your body.
Since you won't be playing or working,
The temperature in your body will go down.

When your temperature gets lower,
You start to feel chilly.
Sometimes if you kick your covers off
In your sleep,
You will wake up and find them.

Sometimes you find them without waking.

When you are relaxed and tired
It feels good to be held.
Someone's warm arms feel good
Because your temperature has gone down
Just a little.

The writer of the psalms wanted to tell us
How much God cared.
So he made up a way we would understand.

He said God cares so much
He covers us with His feathers.
God covers us up.
I understand that.
I feel loved, warm and comfortable
Because I know how much God loves me.

When you pull up your covers tonight,
Remember
God's love for you is just like a warm cover.

"He shall cover thee with his feathers"
(Ps. 91:4, KJV).

Breathing and Sleeping

God made a strange little worm called a larva.
It is almost too tiny to see.
When it becomes an adult
It will be a Hover-fly.

This small worm has a problem.
It lives in a muddy pond.
The Hover-fly worm has to breathe
But it can't in the pond.

To help it out God put a long tail
On the small creature.
The tail sticks up out of the water.
A Hover-fly larva breathes through its tail.

If this sounds strange,
Ask yourself a question.
How can you breathe
After you are asleep?
Why doesn't your chest stop moving
In and out?

We breathe slowly while we sleep.
But our body keeps taking in air.
You don't have to stay awake tonight
To keep breathing.

God started people by breathing air into them.
Tonight our bodies will keep working
Just the way He put them together.

"The time came when the Lord God formed a man's body from the dust of the ground and breathed into it the breath of life. And man became a living person" (Gen. 2:7, TLB).

A Good, Warm Bath

Do you enjoy taking a bath at night?
Are you someone who puts it off
As long as possible?

A warm bath can make you feel clean
And even sleep better.

Keeping clean is a busy job.
Washing hands
And scrubbing behind your neck
And brushing your teeth
Are all important to good health.

Animals like to stay clean also.
The chimpanzee spends hours at it.

Chimpanzees are friendly and help each other.
They pick bugs, seeds and tiny pieces of dirt
Off their brothers, sisters, parents
And children.

They spend an hour each day
Getting checked over.
Sometimes more than one chimp will help.

As a baby chimp grows older
Its mother spends more time
Keeping it clean.

We can clean the outside of our body,

But only God can cleanse us from sin.
When we do something wrong,
God wants to wash away the wrong
And then we can forget it.

**"Create in me a clean heart, O God,
filled with clean thoughts and right
desires"** (Ps. 51:10, TLB).

The Long Sleep

Not every animal sleeps
For just one night or day.
Some sleep for weeks or months
Without once waking up.

This is called hibernating.
It is a deep, deep sleep.
Their bodies become cooler.
Their hearts don't beat as often.
They even breathe less.

Squirrels will hibernate.
This is why we don't usually
See them during the winter.

A squirrel's body slows down.
It doesn't eat or drink for months.
It just takes a long winter nap.

When a ground squirrel hibernates,
It curls up into a ball.
As long as the weather stays cold
It will just keep sleeping.

God made some animals to sleep
For months,
Just as He made you to sleep tonight.
He knows what is best for all of us.

"For all the animals of field and forest are mine! The cattle on a thousand hills! And all the birds upon the mountains!" (Ps. 50:10, 11, TLB).

Everything Ends

It often bothers us
That everything has to end.
We eat cold chocolate ice cream
And after a while it's gone.

We play with our friends,
And when it starts to get dark
We usually have to go home.

Sometimes we are glad things end.
Have you ever had to sit still
And not get out of the chair?
Weren't you glad when it was over?

If you are having a good time,
Like swimming or playing ball,
You don't like to have to come in
And maybe go to bed.

Would you like to live in a place
Where there are many good things to do
And time isn't really important?

Heaven must be this way.
The Bible calls it eternal life.
Eternal means it never ends.
It just goes on and on and on.

"God hath given to us eternal life"
(1 John 5:11, KJV).

Some Things You Can't See

How many things can you name
Which are real and you can't see them?

You can't see the wind.
You can see what it does.
A flag flaps in the wind
Or a kite sails high into the sky.
But you still don't see the wind,
Only what it does.

There are millions of tiny seeds
In the air, flying past.
They are so small you can't see them.
But they are all around us.

Every day and night
Little living things are all around us
And we don't see them.
Some are germs and bacteria.
Some are helpful and some hurt.
You can only see them by using a microscope.

None of us has seen God.
He is all around us but He is invisible.
Thousands of people saw Him
When they saw Jesus Christ.
God can be as close as your hand
Without your seeing Him.

"Who is the image of the invisible
   God, the firstborn of every creature"
(Col. 1:15, KJV).

Can You Sleep, Standing?

Would you enjoy sleeping, standing up?
Could you spend all night
Standing in the middle of the floor
Sound asleep?

A Flamingo is a bird which can.
It even stands on one foot
While it sleeps.

An owl can, too.
It holds tightly to a limb,
Closes its eyes like a child
And sleeps for hours in a tree.

Elephants can sleep most of the night
Standing straight up.
For just a few hours
They lie down on their sides.

A huge rhinoceros can do the same thing.
He weighs more than a ton.
But he can sleep for hours on his feet.
His head hangs down and he looks sad.
He is really only getting some sleep.

People find it more relaxing to lie down.
We get under our covers
And our bodies don't have to work
So hard.

Lying down is a good place to think
About the God who made us,
Watches us,
And loves us.

"I will lie down in peace and sleep, for though I am alone, O Lord, you will keep me safe" (Ps. 4:8, TLB).

Good or Bad?

Are all boys strong?
Are all girls nice?
It really depends on the person.
We are each different.

We talk about people
As if we were all the same.
We say, "Children are noisy,"
Or, "Boys drop everything."
We are each different
And special.

The same is true of bugs.
Some damage trees, bushes
And even buildings.
Others are helpful and save crops.

Once a certain type of bug
Was destroying orange trees in California.
A scientist sent 28 ladybug beetles to America.
They ate the bad bugs and saved the trees.

You are like a bug.
Would you like to be a good bug
Or a bad one?
Do you enjoy causing trouble,
Or do you want to be kind and helpful?

I think you are a good bug.
You like to be nice
To parents, friends, brothers and sisters.
You get to choose to be good or bad.
I think you are a good bug.

"A good man's mind is filled with honest thoughts; an evil man's mind is crammed with lies" (Prov. 12:5, TLB).

Songs in the Night

Do you enjoy music?
Most children seem to.
Do you enjoy records, tapes,
Radios or singing out loud?

While you are sleeping tonight,
Music will probably be playing
Outside your window.

If it is spring or summer,
The musicians play more often.
They have drums, trumpets and singers.

The crickets will play the violins.
They rub their wings together
To make a loud sound.
If there are other crickets around
It plays even louder.

Bullfrogs will take care of the singing.
They enjoy songs so much.
Sometimes if people sing outside,
Bullfrogs will start croaking along with them.

Robins like to sing during the day.
However, just before they fly
To their favorite spot.
There they sing one final song to say,
"Good night."

Close your eyes and listen.
Some place nature's musicians are playing.
Their music sounds
Just the way God wants it to sound.

"But none saith, Where is God my maker, who giveth songs in the night?" (Job 35:10, KJV).

Do You Love?

Whom do you love?
Name someone, maybe two or three.
It is fun to love someone.
It is also fun to be loved.

I wonder if animals love each other?
A fox will take care of its pups,
Train and feed them
Before she lets them go.
This is one way to love.

Does a robin love its new chicks?
Robin parents work hard for their babies.
As long as the chicks keep their beaks open,
The parents search for and carry back
Juicy worms.

Do chickens love their new babies?
After the eggs hatch
The mother opens her wings
And the chicks sleep under her soft feathers.

I don't really know if animals
Love each other the way we do.
But I do know you love.
You prove it by the way you act
And talk and try to help.

Love does things.
It picks up so Mother doesn't have to.

It says, "Thank you."
Love doesn't demand its own way.
Love wants to make other people happy.

Just before you close your eyes
Think of someone you love.
Isn't it great to have that person around?

Good night!

"There are three things that remain —faith, hope, and love—and the greatest of these is love" (1 Cor. 13:13, TLB).

Alligator Nest

Aren't you glad you have a strong home?
The walls don't move.
If it rains, the ceiling won't fall down.
You can sleep tonight
Without worrying about the kitchen
Falling apart.

People need a warm, dry home.
Most animals build a place to live also.
However, they aren't always as well built
And safe as yours.

The alligator has a big job building a home.
It is the mother's job.
She has to gather wet mud in her mouth
And pack it for a nest.

Then she collects rotting grass and weeds
And adds these to the home.
When she is finished
The mud will be packed three feet high.
It is a lot of work when you can use
Only your mouth.

A big nest is necessary.
She will lay 15 eggs—
And maybe 80.
She then covers them over with grass.

You and I are thankful for a good home.
We need it tonight so we can sleep quietly.
But we will always need a place to live
Even after we go to heaven.

Nothing to worry about.
Jesus Christ has made a home for us
In heaven.
We don't know what it looks like.
All we know is that Christ has prepared it.

"There are many homes up there where my Father lives, and I am going to prepare them for your coming" (John 14:2, TLB).

Learning to Share

Would you like to be a parent
When you grow up?
Would you enjoy being a father,
Holding a baby on your knee?
Would you like to be a mother,
Rocking a real baby?

The best parents are the ones
Who have learned to share.
They give food, clothing and games
To their children.

They don't give too much
Because they don't want
To spoil their children.
They give them just enough
Because they love and can share.

Baby robins are small birds
Which need their parents all the time.
These little chicks are big eaters.
Both the mother and father
Have to hunt worms
Just to keep the babies fed.

Sometimes people have trouble sharing.
We want to keep everything.

If someone wants to use the toys or books,
Some children always say "no."

Other children are learning early.
It is nice to share.
It feels good to say "yes."
It is kind to say, "You can use this."

If you share you will make a good parent.
If you share you will make a good person.

"For God so loved the world, that he gave his only begotten Son"
(John 3:16, KJV).

Living in Caves

Caves are dangerous places.
They have deep holes filled with water.
Some have high ledges we could fall from.
They have scary animals and snakes.

It is even worse because caves are so dark.
Often you can't see your hand before your eyes.
Children should never go into a cave
Without an adult.
Even with an adult they had better stay close.

If you do go into a cave with an adult,
There are some amazing things to find:
Tall waterfalls underground,
Long beautiful rocks you can see
With a flashlight.

Of course, there is something you would find
In every cave.
God would be there.
He is always in the darkness
Just as He is always in the light.

Tonight, while you are sleeping,
God will be in that dark cave miles away.
He will also be in your dark room
At the same time.
You can't see Him but He stays close
All the time.

Good night, God!

"He knoweth what is in the darkness" (Dan. 2:22, KJV).

An Animal's Teeth

Did you brush your teeth tonight?
Did you do a good job?
Do you brush your teeth every night?

Teeth are just as important to animals
As they are to people.
They not only need good teeth to eat
But they also use them to hunt
And to protect themselves.

An elephant can't use his two big teeth to eat.
They are called tusks
And are used to dig food out of the ground
Or break branches from trees.

A walrus uses its teeth to fight off enemies.
If a polar bear attacks,
It may find a walrus' teeth too much to handle.

Some animals have no teeth at all.
An anteater sucks its food in
Through its long nose.

Animals don't brush their teeth the way we do.
But some of them may wish they could.
If a bear keeps on eating too much honey,
He may get some painful cavities.
Nobody wants to be near a bear
With a toothache.

God would like to have us brush our teeth.
He wants us to be as healthy as possible.
Night is a great time to brush them.
Then our teeth will be clean for hours.

"Beloved, I wish above all things that
thou mayest prosper and be in
health" (3 John 2, KJV).

The Sun Shines at Midnight

Is it still daylight where you live?
Pretend that tonight
The sun refused to go away.
How would you like the sun to stay bright
Until, maybe, midnight?

During the summer in Alaska
The sun stays up almost all night.
Around 12 p.m. it starts to get dark.
By 3 a.m. the sun is bright again
Just as if it were the middle of the day.

Many people have trouble sleeping
In June and July.
They don't feel like going to sleep
While it is still daylight.

It doesn't get too warm in the summer,
But people enjoy the outdoors.
They can go camping and stay up
Half the night.

Because the days are so long
Food grows extra large.
A little radish is as big as a tomato
In Alaska.
A head of cabbage might weigh 30 pounds.
Cucumbers are as large as a man's forearm.

Maybe you have never seen vegetables
This large,
But you do have many good things.
Can you name two things you are thankful for?
What are they?

God has been good.

"Every good gift and every perfect gift is from above, and cometh down from the Father of lights" (James 1:17, KJV).

94

Someone to Care

It is dangerous to be an animal.
In many ways it sounds like fun
To be as quick as a high-flying eagle.
But there are animals waiting
To hurt each other.

No one has a more dangerous life
Than the Ridley Turtle.
During the late night
A female will come on land
And lay a hundred eggs.

Then the mother leaves them to hatch.
A few babies make it to the sea,
But most are attacked by animals and birds.

Without someone special to care,
Most of these little turtles can't make it.

I'm glad you are not a turtle.
You have someone who cares about you.
Is it a mother, a father, a brother or sister?
Is it an uncle, a grandparent
Or someone who isn't even related?

Tonight thank God for the special someone,
The person God has given to watch over you.

"Whosoever shall receive one of such children in my name, receiveth me"
(Mark 9:37, KJV).

Live in Peace

Ants are much like people.
For some reason they enjoy
Fighting other ants,
Sometimes in large, long wars.

Often a group of red ants
Will attack a hill of black ants.
The fighting is usually terrible
And might last all day.

If the red ants win,
They steal the black ant cocoons
And take them home.
When the baby black ants
Come out of the cocoons,
The red ants make them slaves.

It is a terrible story:
Fighting, stealing, killing, slaves.
Ants are much like people—
Some people fight, hurt and steal.

Would ants be happier if they didn't fight?
I know people would.
No more war or hate,
Or hurting human beings.

Peace is important to God.
He would like to see us
Get along with each other
And love.

Jesus Christ said, "Happy are those who strive for peace—they shall be called the sons of God" (Matt. 6:9, TLB).

Do You Argue?

Sometimes nothing seems to go right.
I know you have had a day like that.
Maybe you get mad at your friends.
Your bike breaks and you yell at it.

But do you ever wonder why
On some other day
Your bike breaks
And you don't get mad?

Maybe your brother takes your game
Without even asking.
But you don't get upset.

One of the reasons we get mad easily
Or upset at little things
Or mad at our brother
Is simply because we didn't get enough sleep.

Doctors have found that people
Without enough sleep
Often argue more
Than those who get enough sleep.

You probably don't like to go to bed.
But one good thing about it—
Tomorrow will go a great deal nicer for you.

"Like cattle grazing in the valleys, so the Spirit of the Lord gave them rest" (Isa. 63:14, TLB).

100

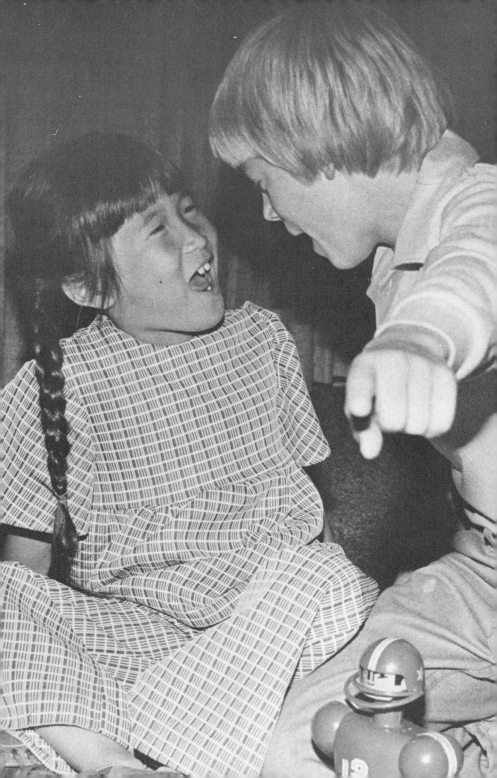

Think of Something Good

Before you go to sleep tonight
Think about something good.
What has happened to you today
That's especially nice?

Stop and name one thing.

We often forget the good people.
We often forget the nice gifts.
We sometimes even forget the good animals.

One of the kindest animals is the dolphin.
He looks a little bit like a shark
But he isn't.

Dolphins like boys, girls and adults.
Even dolphins which are never trained.
They live wild in the ocean
But they still like people.

They will eat out of the hand of a swimmer.
They will pull at your arm like a puppy.
Dolphins act like you are a playmate.
A wild dolphin once gave a young girl a ride
By the ocean.

Don't forget all the good things in life.
Don't forget what people have done for you.
Don't forget what you have done for others.
Don't forget what God has given you.

Again, name one good thing that happened
To you today.

**"Always be full of joy in the Lord;
I say it again, rejoice!** (Phil. 4:4, TLB).

What Is the Milky Way?

It sounds like a candy bar
Or a tall, cold drink.
There is also a large group of stars
Surrounding the earth
Called the Milky Way.

There are many groups of stars
And we can't see them.
In just our group of stars,
There are billions of stars.
There are more stars around the earth
Than you or I could count.

Some of the stars are smaller than the earth.
Most of them are much larger.

If you wanted to visit the closest star,
And you could travel
As fast as any spaceship could go,
It would take you four years
To get to the closest star.

Has anyone ever counted all the stars?
Has anyone ever named all of them?
So far, just one person has.

God knows every star in the sky.
He also knows you and your name.
God knows what time you are going to sleep.
He is going to stand by your bed
And watch your eyes close.

One day God made a star stop
And shine over Bethlehem.
He used it to show
Where Jesus Christ would be born.

"And look! The star appeared to them again, standing over Bethlehem"
(Matt. 2:9, TLB).

106

Seeing in the Dark

Can you see in the dark?
Most of us think we can't.
That is why we like a light on at night.

The truth is, we can see better than we think.
Have you noticed
That after the lights have been out
For a while,
You can start to see things in your room?

Maybe you can start to see
The frame of a picture on the wall.
Maybe you can see part of a chair
Over in the corner.

If we stay in the dark for an hour,
We begin to see fairly well.
A person can see as well as an owl in the dark.
We can see better than a rabbit at night.

If you and I can see this well at night,
Can you imagine how well God can see?
To Him night is just like daylight.
God can see everything and everyone—
Even in the darkest night.

He can see you as if it were lunch time.
When you turn out the light,
God will still see you just as well.

"For even darkness cannot hide from God; to you the night shines as bright as day. Darkness and light are both alike to you" (Ps. 139:12, TLB).

False Heads

Have you noticed the round spots
On a butterfly's wings?
They are a dark color
And might have a white ring around them.

These spots play a big part
In protecting the butterfly.
If a bird starts to attack,
A butterfly will open its wings wide.
The spots look like eyes.
The spread wings look like an animal head.

The bird thought it was attacking a butterfly.
Suddenly it looks like a big animal.
Often the bird will turn and fly away.

The minute the bird becomes frightened
The butterfly will take off
In the other direction.

Do you like to pretend you are someone else?
At night, do you act like
You are a cowboy or a policeman
Or a fireman?
Many children do and it's fun.

Pretending is fun.
Lying is wrong.
I'm glad you can tell the difference.

"Lie not one to another" (Col. 3:9, KJV).

110

What Is a Name?

Where do names come from?
Some animals get their names
From their strange looks
Or the way they live.

The Fiddler Crab got its name
Because it has one huge claw
And one small claw.
He looks like he is playing a violin.

A praying mantis is an insect.
He folds his hands in front of his face
And looks like he is praying.

The night crawler is a long worm.
When we go out in the morning
(Especially after a rain),
We often see them on the ground.

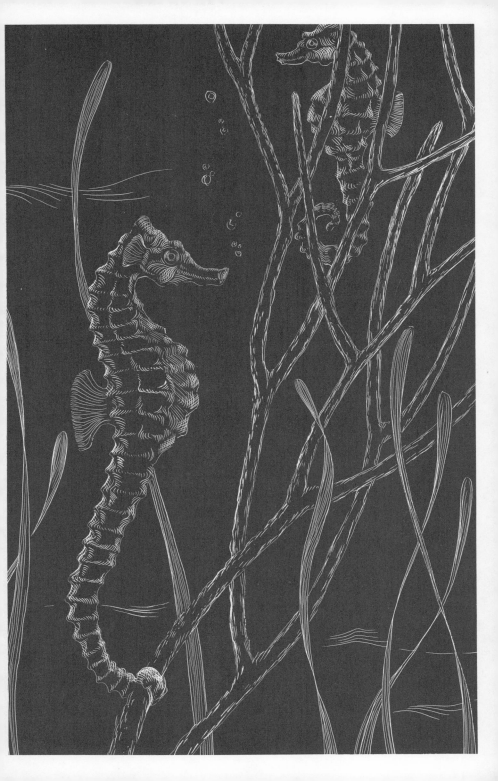

A sea horse isn't a horse at all.
Its head looks like a horse
And it is the only fish to swim
While sitting up straight.

What does Jesus Christ our Lord mean?
Jesus means He wants to help us.
Christ means He is especially selected by God.
Lord means He wants us to obey Him.

"Always give thanks for everything to our God and Father in the name of our Lord Jesus Christ" (Eph. 5:20, TLB).

Moving Quickly

How fast can you run?
You can probably go pretty fast.
The other day I raced my 12-year-old son.
He beat me.

How fast do you travel in a car?
If you are out on the highway,
You probably go about 55 miles
In one hour.

When men traveled to the moon,
They went about 20,000 miles in one hour.
That means they could go
Almost around the world
In just one hour.

The fastest runners in the world
Can run an entire mile
In only four minutes.

People can move quickly.
And we are getting faster
All the time.

One person travels faster than anyone else.
He is Jesus Christ.
Someday He will come back to earth.
When He does He will come quickly.

I don't know how far He has to come,
But He could be here in a split second.

"Surely, I come quickly" (Rev. 22:20, KJV).

A Crab's Shadow

When the sun goes down each evening
Shadows become longer.
Look at your shadow on a sunny evening.
See how tall it is.

If Racing Crabs lived in your area,
You would see something strange.
This crab's shadow would run
Across the ground,
But you couldn't see the crab.

The Racing Crab is the color of the ground.
He is really hard to find.
But you can see his shadow hurry past you.
This is why he is called the ghost crab.

At evening and night there is much activity—
Bugs, animals and birds running
Here and there.
No person could keep up with all that goes on.
Only God can have His eye on everything.

God knows when a baby fox gets lost.
He knows if a sudden storm is coming.
God knows if dew will collect on the grass.
And He knows everything about you.

God is even more interested in people
Than He is in nature.
Sleep in peace tonight.
You are very important to God.

"In my search for wisdom I observed all that was going on everywhere across the earth—ceaseless activity, day and night. (Of course, only God can see everything, and even the wisest man who says he knows everything, doesn't!)" (Eccles. 8:16, 17, TLB).

A Long Lion Sleep

How long can you sleep?
Eight hours? Ten hours? Maybe twelve?

It all depends on how busy
You were today.
It also depends on who you are.
One person needs more sleep
Than someone else.

Lions love to sleep.
They live in small groups called a pride.
They hunt together, clean each other
And protect their friends.

After a lion has had a big meal
He looks for a soft place in the grass.
He then stretches out next to his friends.
In a few minutes they are all sleeping
Like little kittens.

If nothing dangerous comes along,
They will sleep for four days—
That is around 96 hours—
Before waking up.

Tonight you can sleep just like a lion,
Quietly, peacefully, softly.
Stretch out your arms, yawn a little.
Tell God good night.

"Israel sleeps like a lion or a lioness"
(Num. 24:9, TLB).

Who Makes Your Bed?

Chimpanzees make their own bed every night.
They don't like to sleep on the bare ground
Or high in a tree.

Just before dark they start collecting
Branches and leaves.
They make a large pile on the ground.

It is soft and bouncy
Like a comfortable mattress.

His arms and legs are strong.
He breaks branches
Most people would find too thick.
The chimpanzee works for just a few minutes
And his new bed is all ready.

A soft bed is important to him.
He wants a good night's rest.
Tomorrow night Mr. Chimp will build
Another one.

Do you help make your bed?
Do you smooth out your covers?
Do you put your pillow at the top?

A bed is a help to chimpanzees and people.
We keep them neat because they belong to us.

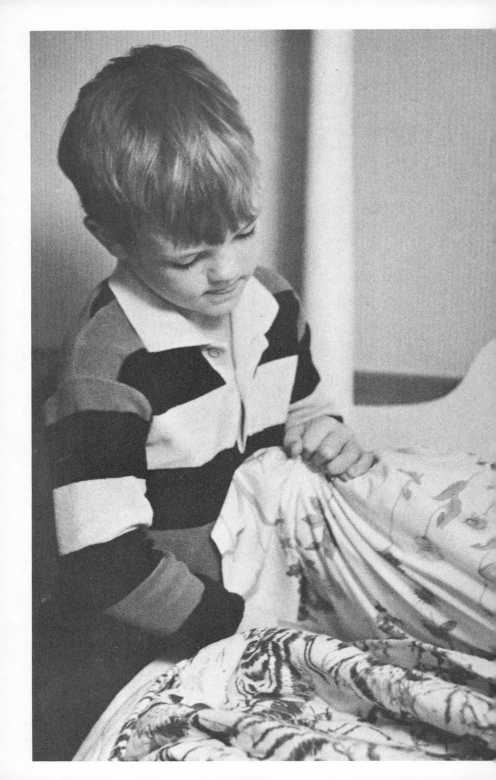

While you are resting on your bed tonight,
Think about the loving God who cares for you.
As you start to close your eyes
Remember all the kind things
He has given you.

"Stand before the Lord in awe, and do not sin against him. Lie quietly upon your bed in silent meditation"
(Ps. 4:4, TLB).

Always Dark

Have you ever played a game
While you were blindfolded?
Maybe it was Pin the Tail on the Donkey
Or guessing what is handed to you.

If you don't want to see,
You can just close your eyes.
Insects can't do that.
They sleep with their eyes open.
But somehow they still don't see.

Most insects can only see things
Which are close to them.
Other insects like the Robber Fly
Can see little bugs flying quickly past.

Insects probably do not see as well
As you do.
When they see a bug
It is fuzzy looking.
They use their taste and feel
More than they use their eyes.

If you can see well,
You can be thankful.
I am thankful for glasses.
Without them I would miss
Most things.

Tonight use your eyes
To look up into the heavens.
Do you see clouds, stars, the moon?
They are the fantastic works of God.

"The heavens declare his righteousness, and all the people see his glory" (Ps. 97:6, KJV).